W9-CMO-701

Learn to DRAW

Drawing
Dinosaurs

Jorge Santillan and Sarah Eason

Gareth Stevens
Publishing

**Please visit our website, www.garethstevens.com. For a free color catalog of all
our high-quality books, call toll free 1-800-542-2595 or fax 1-877-542-2596.**

Library of Congress Cataloging-in-Publication Data

Eason, Sarah.
 Drawing dinosaurs / Sarah Eason.
     pages cm. — (Learn to draw)
ISBN 978-1-4339-9529-3 (pbk.)
ISBN 978-1-4339-9530-9 (6-pack)
ISBN 978-1-4339-9528-6 (library binding)
1. Dinosaurs in art—Juvenile literature. 2. Drawing—Technique—Juvenile literature. I.
Title.
 NC825.D56E27 2013
 743.6—dc23
                                   2012048244

Published in 2014 by
Gareth Stevens Publishing
111 East 14th Street, Suite 349
New York, NY 10003

Produced for Gareth Stevens by Calcium Creative Ltd
Illustrated by Jorge Santillan
Designed by Paul Myerscough
Edited by Rachel Blount

Printed in the United States of America

CPSIA compliance information: Batch CS13GS: For further information contact Gareth Stevens, New York, New York at 1-800-542-2595.

Contents

Learn to Draw!

Millions of years ago, terrifying giants walked across our planet—the dinosaurs! These enormous creatures came in all shapes and sizes, from tiny and quick-footed runners to huge, stalking killers. Some ate plants, and some hunted down other dinosaurs for meat. Discover more about the awesome dinosaurs, from what they ate to how they cared for their babies. Then learn how to draw them, too!

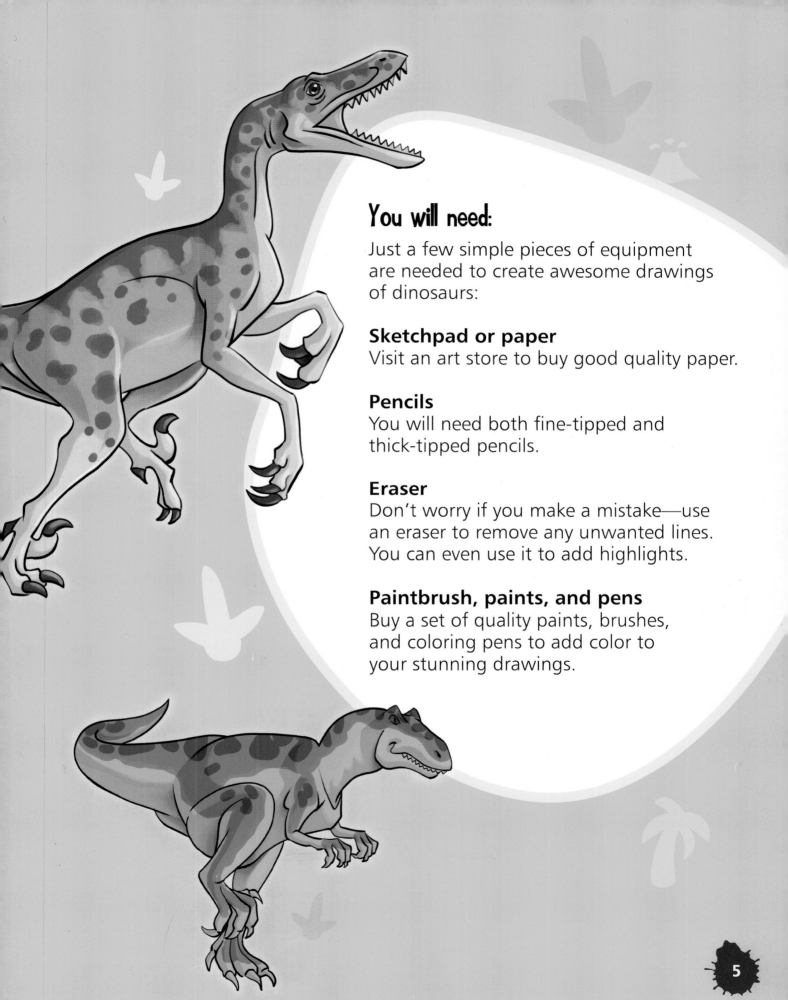

You will need:

Just a few simple pieces of equipment are needed to create awesome drawings of dinosaurs:

Sketchpad or paper
Visit an art store to buy good quality paper.

Pencils
You will need both fine-tipped and thick-tipped pencils.

Eraser
Don't worry if you make a mistake—use an eraser to remove any unwanted lines. You can even use it to add highlights.

Paintbrush, paints, and pens
Buy a set of quality paints, brushes, and coloring pens to add color to your stunning drawings.

Terrifying T-rex

Tyrannosaurus rex means "tyrant lizard king"
and this terrifying hunter lived up to its name!
Also known as *T. rex, Tyrannosaurus rex* was
an enormous meat-eating dinosaur. The giant killer
stalked plant-eating dinosaurs, then killed them with
a powerful bite from its huge, teeth-lined jaws.

Step 1

Draw a rectangle for the
killer's body, then draw its
neck, tail trunk, legs, and
feet. Draw the shape of the
forearms. Then draw the
giant head and a crescent
shape for the tail tip.

Step 2

Draw the shape of the jaws
and the dinosaur's feet and
forearm claws. Mark the eye
and the tail and leg sections.
Erase the rough lines you
drew in step 1.

Step 3

Now add the terrifying teeth, the shape of the powerful jaws, and the inside of the mouth. Pencil the outline of the eye and the ridge above it. Add more detail to the feet.

Step 4

Give your dinosaur its terrifying expression by drawing the lines on the face and around the eye and neck. Then draw the claws on the feet.

Step 5

Shade *T. rex's* body, tail, legs, feet, and forearms. Add shading to its huge head and gaping mouth.

Step 6

Color the back, head, outer legs, forearms, and the top of the tail green. Add dark green spots. Color the underside of the tail, belly, chest, inside front leg, and jaws light green. Add a pink tongue and an angry, orange eye.

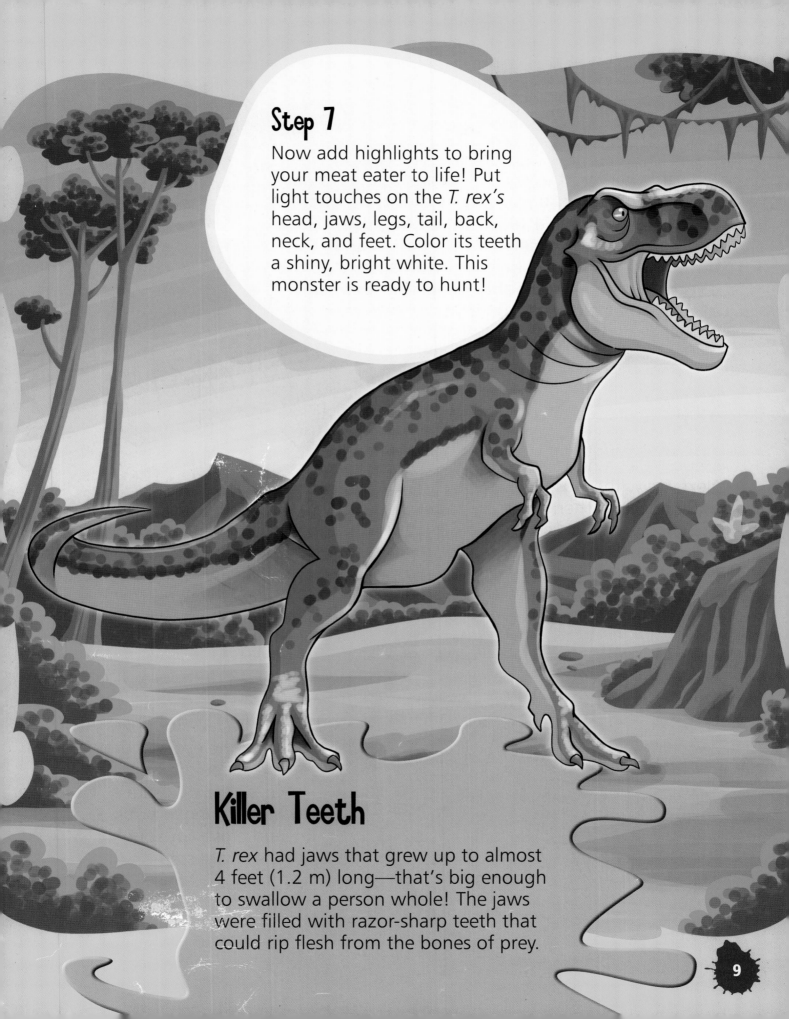

Step 7

Now add highlights to bring your meat eater to life! Put light touches on the *T. rex's* head, jaws, legs, tail, back, neck, and feet. Color its teeth a shiny, bright white. This monster is ready to hunt!

Killer Teeth

T. rex had jaws that grew up to almost 4 feet (1.2 m) long—that's big enough to swallow a person whole! The jaws were filled with razor-sharp teeth that could rip flesh from the bones of prey.

Spiny Stegosaurus

The plant eater *Stegosaurus* had a row of huge, bony spines along its back. This gentle giant may have used the spines to protect itself from meat eaters. The dinosaur also had sharp, pointed spines at the end of its tail. It probably used them to stab at any meat eaters that came too close.

Step 1

Draw a large oval for the *Stegosaurus*'s huge body. Next, draw the legs, neck, and tail trunk. Then draw the head and a crescent for the tip of the tail. Add lines for the spines.

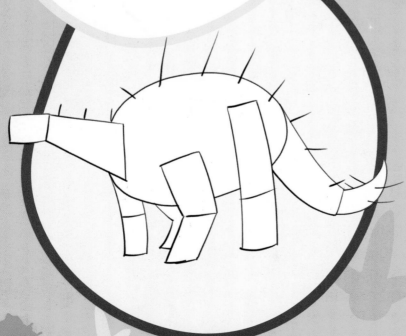

Step 2

Now add the shape of the spines and the spikes on the tail. Roughly mark the eye and draw the shape of the jaws. Give your dinosaur a more rounded outline and erase any rough lines from step 1.

Step 3

Draw the outline of the eye and draw the claws on the dinosaur's feet.

Step 4

Now add more detail to the eye and jaws. Draw the muscle lines on the dinosaur's body and legs. Add detail to the claws.

Step 5

Shade the dinosaur's huge body and powerful tail. Add shading to the head and spines.

Step 6

Color the dinosaur's spines dark purple. Use a slightly lighter purple shade for the top of the back, neck, head, and tail. Use lighter shades of purple for the rest of the dinosaur. Add some dark purple spots.

Step 7

Add a bright blue oval to each of the dinosaur's spines. Color the claws white and add a touch of white to the eye. Add highlights to complete your spiny monster.

Warming Up

Some scientists think that *Stegosaurus* may have used its spines to warm itself up. The dinosaur may have stood with its spines facing the sun to catch the warm rays. The spines would then have warmed up the dinosaur's body—a little like a radiator!

Giant Diplodocus

Enormous *Diplodocus* was one of the biggest creatures ever to walk on Earth! This super-giant measured 90 feet (27 m) long—that's as long as two buses! Its neck was an amazing 26 feet (8 m) long and its tail stretched an incredible 45 feet (14 m) behind the dinosaur's body.

Step 1

Use an oval shape for the dinosaur's huge body. Then draw its legs and long tail. Draw *Diplodocus*'s enormous neck and use a rectangular shape for its head.

Step 2

Next, draw a more rounded outline for your dinosaur and mark the eye and the sections of the legs, tail, and neck.

Step 3

Erase the rough lines from steps 1 and 2. Then roughly draw the dinosaur's face and claws.

Step 4

Now add more detail to the face, neck, and claws. Draw the lines on the body, tail, and legs.

Step 5

Shade the giant's tail, body, legs, and face. Then add shading to the huge neck.

Step 6

Color your dinosaur's belly, inner legs, and the underside of the tail and neck beige. Use a light green for the rest of the dinosaur. Use a darker shade on the top of the back, head, snout, and for the dinosaur's spots.

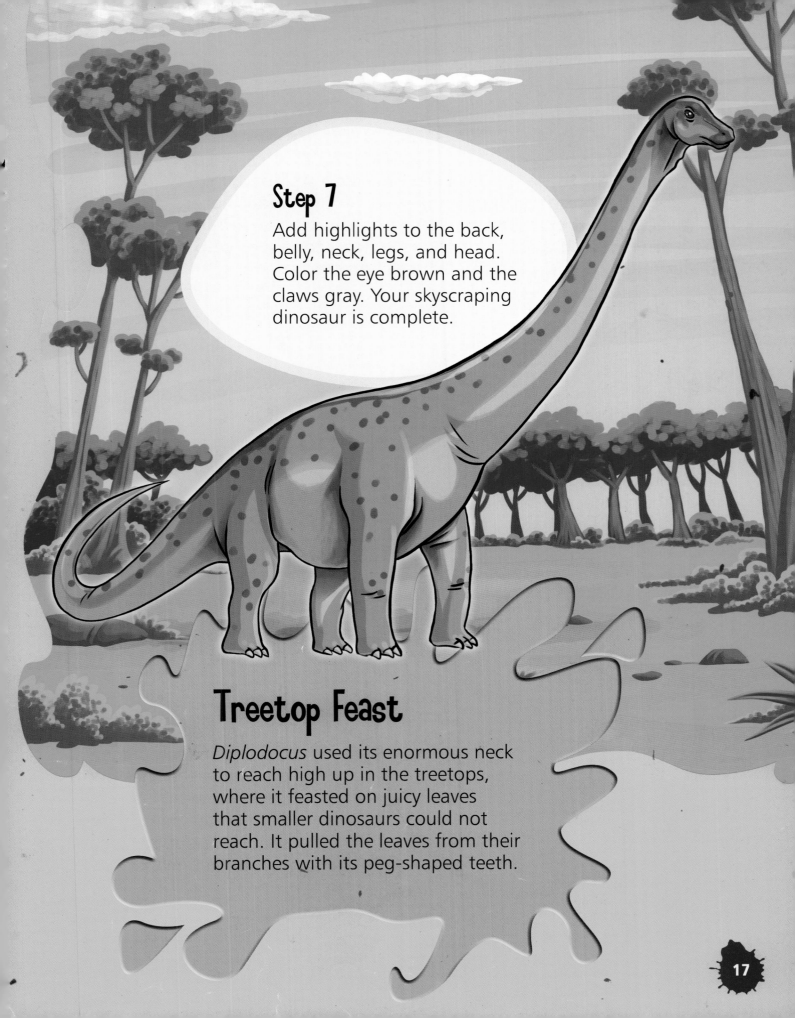

Step 7

Add highlights to the back, belly, neck, legs, and head. Color the eye brown and the claws gray. Your skyscraping dinosaur is complete.

Treetop Feast

Diplodocus used its enormous neck to reach high up in the treetops, where it feasted on juicy leaves that smaller dinosaurs could not reach. It pulled the leaves from their branches with its peg-shaped teeth.

Horned Triceratops

With three razor-sharp horns on its head, *Triceratops* could take on a giant meat eater and win! The plant-eating dinosaur used the horns to stab at any attackers. Triceratops was also protected by a tough, bony "shield" around its neck.

Step 1

Draw the dinosaur's large, powerful body. Then draw the legs and tail. Add the head, horns, and the neck shield that protected the dinosaur from attackers.

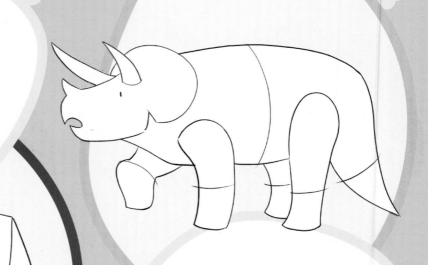

Step 2

Give your dinosaur a more rounded outline, then erase the lines from step 1. Draw the smaller horn on the dinosaur's snout, the outline of its mouth, and mark its eye.

Step 3

Draw the frilly edge of the neck shield, the outline of the eyes, and the "beaky" mouth. Mark the nostril and draw the claws on the feet.

Step 4

Add the triangular shapes at the edge of the neck shield. Pencil the detail of the right eye, then shade the nostril, and draw the lines on the body, legs, and tail.

Step 5

Now add shading to your dinosaur to begin to bring it to life. Use deeper shading around the neck, belly, and the underside of the tail.

Step 6

Use two shades of blue for your dinosaur. Use gray for the horns and purple for the markings on the back and body. Add the two orange circles on the neck shield. Put a small yellow circle within the orange circle on the right.

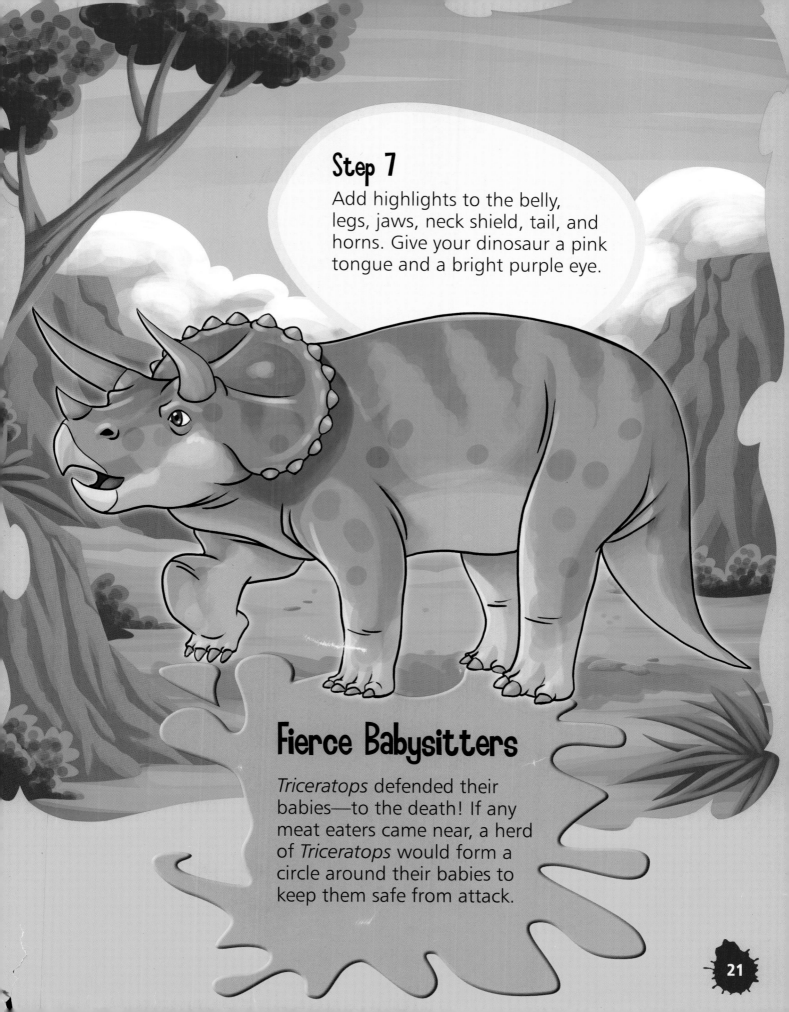

Step 7

Add highlights to the belly, legs, jaws, neck shield, tail, and horns. Give your dinosaur a pink tongue and a bright purple eye.

Fierce Babysitters

Triceratops defended their babies—to the death! If any meat eaters came near, a herd of *Triceratops* would form a circle around their babies to keep them safe from attack.

Deadly Velociraptor

This fierce meat eater was much smaller than giants such as *T. rex*, but it was just as deadly! *Velociraptor* was a smart dinosaur that hunted in packs. A group of these fast-running hunters worked together to bring down large plant eaters, then feasted on them!

Step 1

Draw the body, legs, feet, neck, trunk of the tail, and head of your dinosaur. Use a crescent shape for the tip of the tail.

Step 2

Go over the rough lines from step 1 to give your hunter a curved outline. Roughly mark the eye. Erase the rough lines you drew in step 1.

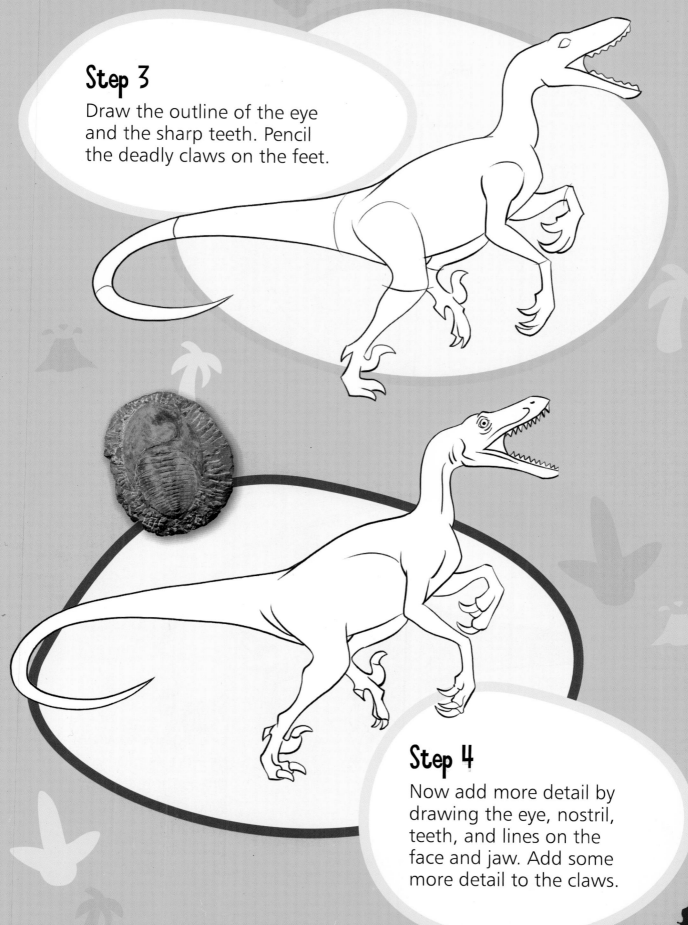

Step 3

Draw the outline of the eye and the sharp teeth. Pencil the deadly claws on the feet.

Step 4

Now add more detail by drawing the eye, nostril, teeth, and lines on the face and jaw. Add some more detail to the claws.

23

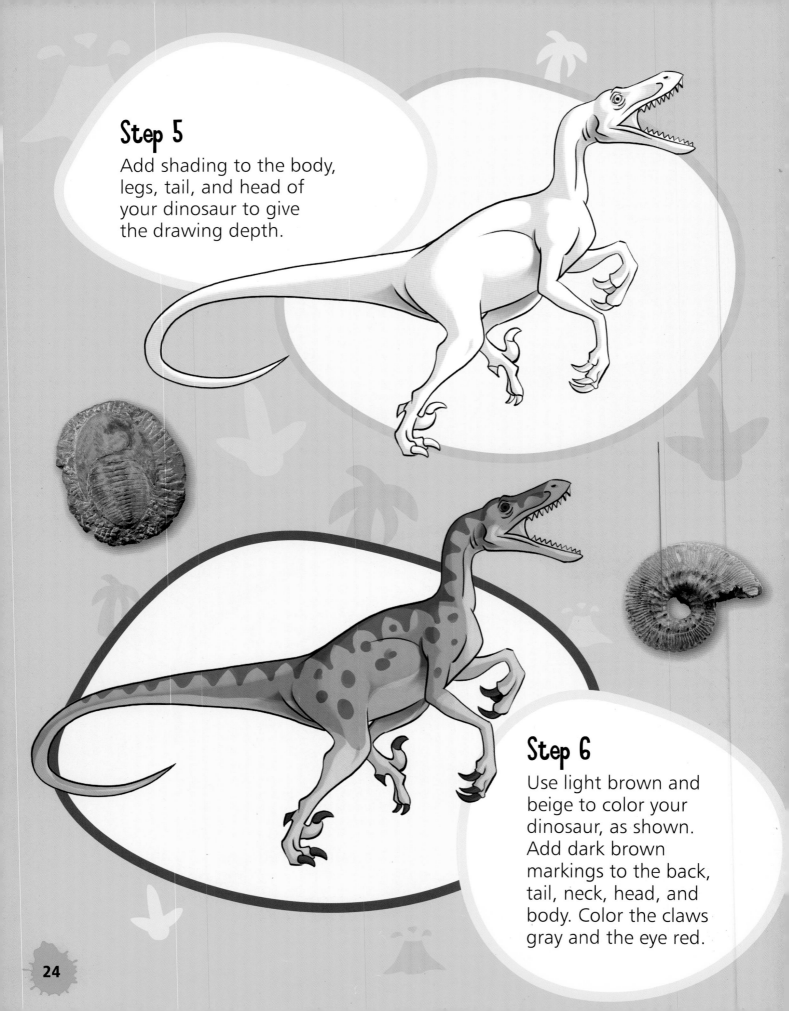

Step 5

Add shading to the body, legs, tail, and head of your dinosaur to give the drawing depth.

Step 6

Use light brown and beige to color your dinosaur, as shown. Add dark brown markings to the back, tail, neck, head, and body. Color the claws gray and the eye red.

24

Step 7

Add highlights to the killer's body, neck, head, eye, and claws. Color the inside of its mouth pale pink. Your scary pack hunter is complete.

Killer Claws

Velociraptor had an incredibly large, sharp claw on its foot. The claw could swivel in almost a complete circle to rip into the flesh of the dinosaur's prey. The hunter used its deadly claw to kill its prey with a lethal slash.

Awesome Allosaurus

Like the mighty *T. rex, Allosaurus* was a giant meat-eating monster. The dinosaur had a bony ridge along its huge head, which held up to 50 enormous, flesh-ripping teeth. *Allosaurus* was one of the biggest and fiercest of all meat-eating dinosaurs.

Step 1

Draw the hunter's huge body and powerful rear legs. Then add the giant neck and head. Draw the strong tail and add the killer's smaller forearms.

Step 2

Go over the rough lines from step 1 and give your dinosaur a rounded outline. Mark the eye and line of the mouth. Erase the rough lines you drew in step 1.

Step 3

Begin to add detail by drawing the outline of the eye, the "horns" on the head, and the outline of the claws. Add the jagged outline of the dinosaur's teeth and a mark for its nostril.

Step 4

Now bring your *Allosaurus* to life by drawing its eye, teeth, and claws in detail.

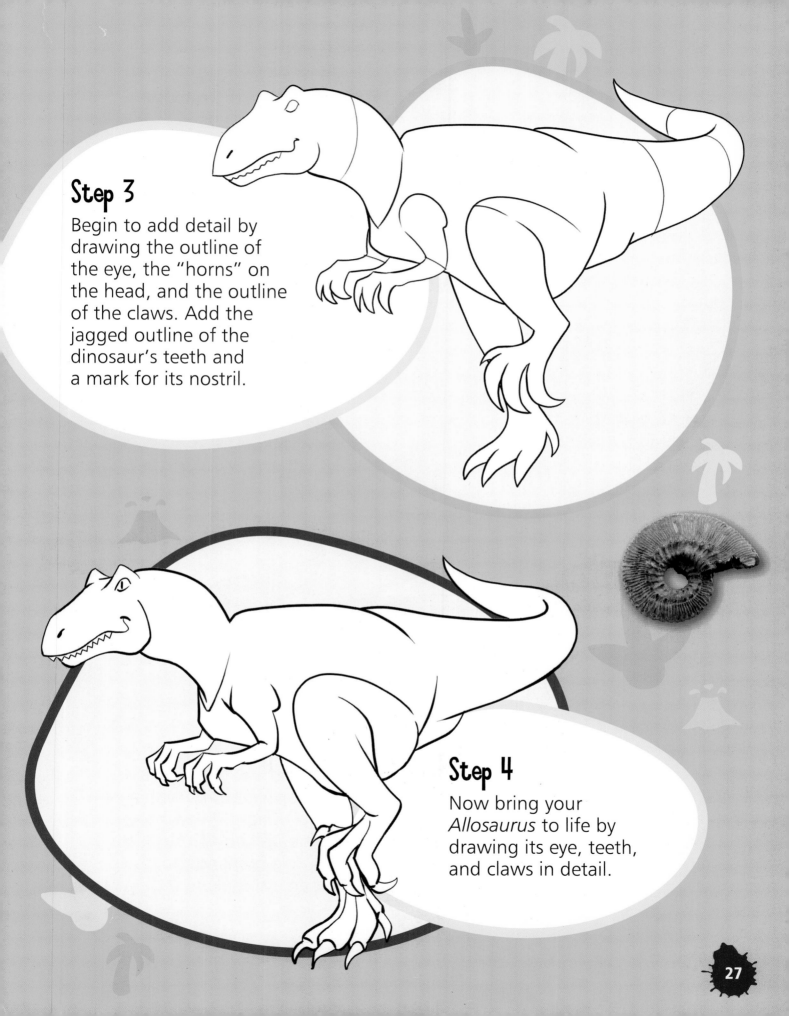

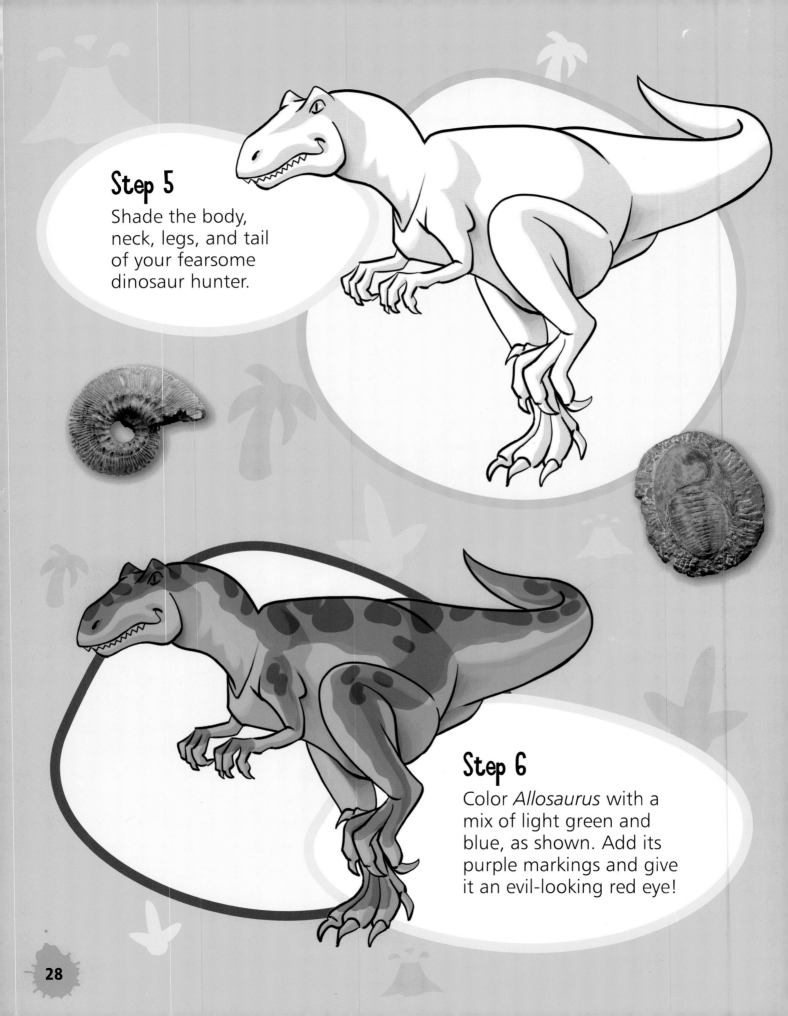

Step 5

Shade the body, neck, legs, and tail of your fearsome dinosaur hunter.

Step 6

Color *Allosaurus* with a mix of light green and blue, as shown. Add its purple markings and give it an evil-looking red eye!

Step 7

Add lots of highlights, and color the teeth white and the claws gray. Then add a dab of white to the dinosaur's eye to complete its scary stare!

Huge Hunter

Allosaurus grew up to 36 feet (11 m) long and weighed up to 2.2 tons (2 mt). The giant killer gripped its prey with its powerful jaws, then threw its head back and forth to rip off big chunks of flesh.

Glossary

attack to try to hurt or kill something

beaky like the hard part on a bird's face

claw a hard, sharp point on a creature's foot

crescent a long, curved shape that looks a little like a half moon

deadly able to kill

defended protected, kept safe

detail the fine lines on a drawing

dinosaurs cold-blooded creatures that lived on Earth millions of years ago

erase to remove

feasted ate

forearms the arms at the front of a creature's body. Meat-eating dinosaurs often had small forearms in comparison to their powerful rear legs.

highlights the light parts on a picture

horns sharp points on a creature's head

hunter a creature that tracks down animals for food

jaws the area of a creature's head in which the teeth are found

lethal can kill

lizard a cold-blooded, scaly creature

nostril an opening on an animal's head through which it breathes

packs groups

prey a creature that is eaten by another for food

ridge a raised hard, bony feature on a creature's body

shading the dark markings on a picture

slash to cut or rip open

spines bony shapes on a creature's back

stalking tracking a creature with the intention of hurting it or killing it

swivel to turn around

tyrant a dangerous ruler

For More Information

Books

Bergin, Mark. *How to Draw Dinosaurs and Other Prehistoric Creatures*. New York, NY: PowerKids Press, 2008.

McKurry, Kristen. *How to Draw Incredible Dinosaurs*. Mankato, MN: Capstone Press, 2012.

Miller, Steve. *Dinosaurs: How to Draw Thunder Lizards and Other Prehistoric Beasts*. New York, NY: Watson-Guptill, 2008.

Websites

Find out more fascinating facts about the dinosaur world at:
www.enchantedlearning.com/subjects/dinosaurs/dinos

Discover incredible facts about the dinosaurs and play cool games, too, at:
www.kidsdinos.com

Visit the Natural History Museum to find out what dinosaurs looked like, where they lived, and why they died out at:
www.nhm.ac.uk/kids-only/dinosaurs/index

Index